RIPE CONDITIONS

A Play

by

CLAUDIA ALLEN

Dramatic Publishing
Woodstock, Illinois • London, England • Melbourne, Australia

*** NOTICE ***

Cover design by Susan Carle.
Cover photo by Suzanne Plunkett. *Used by permission.*
Victory Gardens Theater production, Chicago, featuring (l. to r.)
Linda Kimbrough (Ann), Larry Neumann Jr. (Lester)
and John Judd (Buster).

ISBN 0-87129-485-0

For my teachers:
Jean and Forrest Meek,
Dr. Peter Bauland,
and Dr. Daniel Fader

RIPE CONDITIONS premiered in the summer of 1992 at Stage West in Fort Worth, Texas, Buckley Sachs, director; Jerry Russell, artistic director; with:

Buster . . . . Ron Quade
Lester . . . . Randall Bonifay
Ann . . . . Cheryl Norris

RIPE CONDITIONS had its second professional production in the summer of 1993 at Victory Gardens Theater in Chicago, Illinois; Sandy Shinner, director; Dennis Zacek, artistic director; with:

Buster . . . . John Judd
Lester . . . . Larry Neumann, Jr.
Ann . . . . Linda Kimbrough

RIPE CONDITIONS had its third professional production in the summer of 1993 at the Lois Pope Theatre in Manalapan, Florida; J. Barry Lewis, director; Louis Tyrrell, producing director; with:

Buster . . . . Robert Elliott
Lester . . . . Gordon McConnell
Ann . . . . Sherry Skinker

RIPE CONDITIONS had its fourth professional production in 1994 at the California Cottage Theatre; Roy Brocksmith, director; Roy Brocksmith, artistic director; with:

Buster . . . . Michael Liscio
Lester . . . . Michael Lebeau
Ann . . . . Ruth Cordell

The author thanks all involved in these initial productions for their creative silliness.

RIPE CONDITIONS

A Play in Two Acts
For Two Men and One Woman

CHARACTERS

BUSTER .... a middle-aged rural American

LESTER .... his brother

ANN .... the object of their affections

TIME: Tornado season.

PLACE: A home gone to seed in rural Michigan.

ACT ONE

SCENE: *A messy, musty old farmhouse.*

AT RISE: *LESTER is sitting hunched up by the Blaze Princess—a woodburning stove—with an old Indian blanket wrapped around his shoulders and head. He is slurping a mug of hot tea. With a slam of the door, BUSTER enters.*

BUSTER. Jesus Christ, it's like a goddamn oven in here. What's the matter with you?

LESTER. I'm just trying to get warm.

BUSTER. For cryin' out loud, it's seventy-eight degrees outside. How the hell warm do you need to be?

LESTER. I've got a cold. Is that my fault?

BUSTER. Sure it's your fault. You don't take care of yourself. *(He is at the refrigerator.)* Want a beer?

LESTER *(sniffs)*. I take lots better care of myself than you do, and you've never been sick a day in your life.

BUSTER. You know what your problem is?

LESTER. I suppose you're going to tell me.

BUSTER. You know what your problem is?

LESTER *(sets down his mug)*. All right, what? What is my problem?

BUSTER. You take too many baths.

LESTER. I had to ask.

BUSTER. No, I mean it. I'm serious here. I don't take no more than one bath a month, especially in cold weather.

Take your clothes off as often as you do, no wonder you got a cold. *(He sits with his beer.)*

LESTER. I thought you were going to bring me a beer.

BUSTER. Did you want one?

LESTER. Yes, I want one.

BUSTER. I'm not a mind reader you know. *(He gets up to get LESTER the beer.)*

LESTER. Raymond Bailey called to ask when you were going to take him back his lawn mower. He says his wife drove by yesterday and saw it sitting out in the yard in a foot of grass getting rained on. He said, "Tell that son of a bitch I'm not lendin' him one more thing."

BUSTER. I ran outa gas.

LESTER. Well, you could put that mower on the porch out of the rain. Not everybody likes rust as well as you do.

BUSTER. Maybe I'll siphon some gas outa your pickup an' put it in that mower. Soon as I finish my beer.

LESTER. Siphon some out of your own pickup.

BUSTER. Jesus, you're too sick to leave the house, aren't ya? I got places to go.

LESTER. You're not leaving me stranded out here with no gas while you go to that funeral. Forget that. I'm going, too.

BUSTER. You can't go to a funeral lookin' like that. You look like a goddamn papoose. *(LESTER blows his nose.)* And that. Listen to that. You're gonna go to that funeral 'n' blow your nose like that right in the middle of the service? That's truly disgusting.

LESTER. I'm going, Bus, so you can just give up right now. I'm going, too.

BUSTER. She's not gonna look twice at you if she comes. You know that? If she does look twice, it'll be a doubletake *(Mimes a doubletake as he says this.)* 'cause you look like jackshit.

LESTER. At least I don't stink. You smell so bad she won't want to get within ten feet of you.

BUSTER. I'm gonna smell fine at that funeral. First chance I get, I'm gonna get out the tub. Today's my bath day.

LESTER. I'll just bet it is.

BUSTER. It is.

LESTER. Tell me I bathe too much, then you tell me today—the day before the funeral—is your "bath day"?

BUSTER. Well, it is. Today's the fifteenth, isn't it? Where's the calendar? *(He gets out of his chair.)*

LESTER. I don't know if I'd be wanting to take a bath today if I was you, Buster. I was listening to the radio and they said there's gonna be a tornado watch the next couple days. They said, "Conditions are ripe" for a tornado. If a tornado hit while you were in that tub, you'd be a dead man.

BUSTER *(rummaging)*. Where's that calendar we got from the Farm Bureau people?

LESTER. It rained so hard last night, is there any water in the cellar? If there's a tornado, we shouldn't have water in the cellar.

BUSTER. Who said we were gonna have a tornado? *(Mutters.)* Jesus.

LESTER. The radio. They said, "Conditions are ripe."

BUSTER. I know. I'll check the *TV Guide.* That's got dates in it. *(He walks over to TV to thumb through a mound of* TV Guides.*)*

LESTER. I'm serious about that cellar. If I have to stand in knee-deep water during a tornado with this cold, I am gonna catch pneumonia and die.

BUSTER. Promises, promises. *(Rummaging, he picks up a* TV Guide.*)* Nineteen sixty-nine. I think we could throw this away.

LESTER *(drops his blanket, rises stiffly).* If you won't check that cellar I'm going to.

BUSTER. You better get outa that chair. We gotta spray those beans this week. *We.* I'm not gonna keep breakin' my back doin' all the work around here then keep lettin' you pocket half the proceeds. You and me are gonna spray those beans.

LESTER. Beans.

BUSTER. Well, it is mostly.

LESTER. You're gonna get caught one of these days. *(LESTER is moving a throw rug aside; there's a trapdoor under it.)*

BUSTER. What's wrong with growin' a little cash crop?

LESTER. I'da thought one trip to Jackson Prison would be enough for you.

BUSTER. Why don't you ever buy a new *TV Guide,* for chrissakes? We prob'ly been missin' all sortsa good shows.

LESTER. It's illegal, and you're gonna get caught one of these days.

BUSTER. What's illegal? Buyin' a new *TV Guide* once or twice a year?

LESTER. You know what I'm talking about. I'm talking about what you've really got growing in our beanfield.

BUSTER. Lester, where the hell's your sense of adventure?

LESTER *(pulling up trapdoor, peers down).* Oh, geez, will you look at that. The water's almost up to the canned peaches.

BUSTER. Maybe it drowned a few of the rats.

LESTER *(peering down)*. Nope. I see a couple of 'em down there swimmin'. It's a regular Holiday Inn for rats down there.

BUSTER. For cryin' out loud close that door.

LESTER *(drops the door to close it)*. We better get that pumped out before the tornado comes.

BUSTER. "We"?

LESTER. Well, I can hold the trapdoor while you pump.

BUSTER. Sorry, Les, but "we" can't do it. Pump's broke.

LESTER. Why am I not surprised?

BUSTER. Maybe Raymond Bailey'd let me borrow his.

LESTER. Somehow I doubt it.

BUSTER. I know. I'll take him some peach preserves.

LESTER. Mom canned those.

BUSTER. So?

LESTER. Well, Mom's been dead twelve years; you think they're still okay?

BUSTER. The rats like 'em. Say, I know. I could take him a chicken. A nice, juicy chicken.

LESTER. You are not taking him one of my chickens. Those chickens are not for eating.

BUSTER. Jesus, you'n your goddamn chickens. Next thing you'll be adopting the rats. You'll be givin' 'em names an' knittin' 'em little rat sweaters.

LESTER. You know it's your fault we've got rats in the cellar.

BUSTER. How do you figure that, you asshole?

LESTER. You clean your deer down there, and you never half clean up. No wonder we got rats. Last fall I slid half-way across the cellar on a pile of deer innards. Buster, that sorta thing attracts rats.

BUSTER. I didn't see you turnin' up your nose when I fried us up that venison.

LESTER. All I'm sayin' is you could clean up better.

BUSTER. Jesus, you already got me mowin' the lawn 'n' pumpin' out the goddamn cellar for some tornado the radio's worried about. You're gonna work me to death.

LESTER. Well, I'd do more if I felt better.

BUSTER. You never feel better!

LESTER. Is that my fault?

BUSTER. Here we go.

LESTER. You know I've never been the same since I was in the hospital.

BUSTER. Am I gonna have to hear about that today?

LESTER. Enough said.

BUSTER. Been enough said for years, but that hasn't stopped you.

LESTER. Do you think they'll be there? At the funeral? Her 'n' him both?

BUSTER. Gonna be interestin' to see, isn't it?

LESTER. Do you think she'll know us?

BUSTER. She'll know me.

LESTER. Not clean she won't.

BUSTER. You think we'll know her?

LESTER. I'll know her.

BUSTER. She mighta lost a leg or had face cancer or somethin'.

LESTER. Well, that's possible.

BUSTER. She could even be dead. She could.

LESTER. That's right. Look on the bright side.

BUSTER. Think she's still pretty?

LESTER. Uh huh.

BUSTER. You still think of her?

LESTER. All the time.

BUSTER. Me too.

LESTER. Knowing you, prob'ly in the bathroom. *(Poignant pause.)* I hope she comes.

BUSTER. It's her brother's funeral. Of course, she'll come.

LESTER. I just hope she don't wear a wig.

BUSTER. I'm gonna go mow that lawn.

LESTER. Use your own gas. *(He sneezes, graphically blows his nose into a handkerchief.)*

BUSTER. You better not do that at the funeral or you're headed straight back to the hospital.

LESTER. You just remember what happened to you the last time you pulled that shit.

BUSTER. Yeah. *(Pause.)* An' it was worth it.

LESTER. Go mow your grass.

BUSTER. Maybe if I get his lawnmower back to him today Raymond Bailey'll let me have his pump.

LESTER. Raymond Bailey wouldn't let you use his toilet if your life depended on it.

BUSTER. You'd think the guy never borrowed anything from us.

LESTER. He *doesn't.* Bring me some wood for the Blaze Princess, will you? When you get a chance?

BUSTER. Jesus Christ, it's seventy-eight degrees outside.

LESTER. I gotta boil this cold outa my system, don't I?

BUSTER. Seventy-eight degrees out and he's burnin' wood. We run outa wood this winter, you remember whose fault it is. *(With that, he exits.)*

LESTER *(hollering after him).* Keep your hands off my gas cap! *(Settles back down in his blanket by the stove.)* I gotta get to feelin' better for that funeral. I don't want her mistakin' me for the corpse. *(He holds out his tongue, looks down at it.)* I just hope she's held up better than we have.

SCENE TWO

AT RISE: *There is a large metal tub near the Blaze Princess. A bare BUSTER is in it, soaping his armpit. LESTER, still draped in Indian blanket, pours a large, ancient teakettle full of very hot water into the tub near BUSTER's bottom.*

BUSTER. Jesus, you could warn a guy. You scalded my ass.

LESTER *(miffed)*. You're very welcome. Get your own water after this.

BUSTER. That water was boiling hot.

LESTER. Well, it's got to be or you're never going to come clean.

BUSTER *(sudsing)*. You know, I just don't see it.

LESTER. See what?

BUSTER. What you see in this bathing.

LESTER. It wouldn't be so much work if you'd do it a little more often.

BUSTER. I just don't see it. *(We hear a car pulling up outside.)*

LESTER. Is that a car outside?

BUSTER. How should I know? Look out the window why don'tcha? *(There's a knock at the door.)*

LESTER. Guess I was right. Was a car.

BUSTER. Wonder who it is?

LESTER *(making no move to answer the door)*. Yeah, I wonder.

BUSTER. Funny they didn't call.

LESTER. Maybe they wanted to surprise us. *(Another knock.)*

BUSTER. Prob'ly just somebody wantin' to buy eggs.

LESTER. Oh, yeah. Bet you're right. *(A last, insistent knock.)*

BUSTER. Well, are you gonna answer it or am I gonna have to? *(Makes a move to rise out of the tub.)*

LESTER *(stands with arms folded across his chest, blanket slipping)*. Go ahead.

BUSTER *(through gritted teeth)*. Lester, get the goddamn door.

LESTER. Ask nicely.

BUSTER *(after a furious pause)*. Please get the goddamn door.

LESTER. Okedokee. *(He answers the door.)*

(A WOMAN has just started to walk away.)

ANN. Oh. I was afraid no one was home.

LESTER. What d'ya want?

ANN. I'm afraid I seem to be a little lost. *(BUSTER is staring at her, but LESTER is oblivious. ANN can't see past LESTER to see BUSTER.)*

LESTER. You're lost, huh?

ANN. Yes, I'm afraid so. I was on Route 72 and I thought it would take me right into town, but I must have done something wrong.

LESTER. You know what your problem is, don't you?

ANN. Well, no I don't. Uh, don't I—*(She is about to say, "know you" but LESTER keeps talking.)*

LESTER. Your problem is they rerouted Route 72 about fifteen years ago. *(BUSTER is trying to creep out of the tub, but he can't quite reach a towel or his stack of clean clothes. LESTER continues, oblivious.)* They shaved off a hill and straightened out a stretch where people kept getting themselves killed.

BUSTER *(hisses quietly)*. Lesss-ter. *(ANN hears something but doesn't make out the name.)*

LESTER *(drones on, oblivious)*. You need to go back about two miles to a barn with a "Mail Pouch Tobacco" ad painted on the side, and you need to veer right. You veered left, and you need to veer right.

ANN. Thank you. I am relieved. I was afraid for a minute I'd driven into the Twilight Zone. *(Of course, she has.)*

LESTER *(looks past her)*. Nice car.

BUSTER *(hissing, half-hanging from the tub in an effort to get at his clothing)*. Lester. *(ANN still can't quite hear BUSTER. LESTER ignores him.)*

LESTER *(still looking out at the car)*. Looks new.

ANN. It's not, but I try to keep it up. Could I ask you something?

LESTER. I don't see why not.

ANN. Are you—You aren't—

BUSTER. Lesss-ter.

LESTER *(looks around at BUSTER)*. Look, we got us a lost lady. *(To ANN.)* I think he wants to meet you.

BUSTER. Ohmygod! *(He sinks as much of himself into the small tub as he can and covers his face with his hands.)*

LESTER. That's not what needs covering. *(BUSTER drops his hands into the water to his crotch.)*

ANN *(looks in shyly)*. Hello? I didn't mean to intrude. *(Seeing BUSTER, an electric moment of eye contact.)* Oh my.

BUSTER. Jesus God.

LESTER. Bus, if you didn't wanna meet her, why'd you keep saying, "Lester"?

ANN *(lets out breath)*. Oh my God.

LESTER. What? What? *(A pause. BUSTER and ANN are just looking at each other.)*

BUSTER. Hello, Ann.

ANN. Hello, Buster. Lester? *(It takes LESTER a minute to finally catch on, and even then he can't believe it.)*

LESTER. Naw.

BUSTER. Oh yeah.

LESTER. Naw.

BUSTER. Lester, it's her. Take off that goddamn blanket an' hold it up in front of me.

ANN. I'd be glad to turn around.

BUSTER. Oh, don't bother yourself, Ann. Lester, hold that blanket up in front of me this minute or you're a dead man.

ANN. You two still don't get along?

BUSTER *(pleasantly)*. Oh, better'n we used to. *(Through gritted teeth.)* Lester. *(LESTER finally takes off his blanket and holds it up as a curtain in front of the tub and BUSTER, all the while keeping his eyes glued on ANN.)*

LESTER. You came. I wondered if you would.

ANN. Al was all the family I had left. I never liked him, but I decided the least I could do was help bury him.

BUSTER *(from behind blanket)*. That sounds just like you, Ann. You always were sweet. Wasn't she, Les?

LESTER. Sweet.

ANN *(looking around)*. You know, I thought this might be your place, but I got so twisted around I wasn't sure. But I did wonder when I saw those refrigerators tipped over in the front yard. Good Lord, it's been ages since I saw you boys.

BUSTER. Les was in the hospital. An' me I was—

LESTER. In prison.

ANN. I'm really glad to see you're both okay.

LESTER. Oh yeah. We're fine.

BUSTER *(from behind the blanket)*. Couldn't be better.

ANN. That's great.

LESTER. You musta done well for yourself, Ann. That's a nice car. And that's a real pretty outfit you got on.

ANN. Why thank you. *(BUSTER, more or less dressed, pulls down the blanket, almost pulling LESTER down with it.)*

BUSTER. There. Now I can be part of the conversation, too, huh? Jesus, you do look swell, Ann.

ANN. Well my, so do you. You look so clean.

BUSTER. Oh yeah. I'm always tellin' Les he oughta bathe more.

LESTER. Ann, could I get you a cup of coffee?

ANN. Well, it's a little hot for coffee...

BUSTER. You ignoramus. *(To ANN.)* Him not you. Lester, don't we have any lemonade or ice tea?

LESTER. I think we do have a coupla lemons.

BUSTER. Well then, why don't you get 'em an' make Ann some lemonade.

LESTER. They're in the cellar.

BUSTER. So go get the goddamn th—*(He remembers.)* Are they above or below the peach preserves?

LESTER. Above, but all the way across the cellar.

ANN. If it's a problem...

BUSTER. Hell, no problem. I'll just go get my hip boots. *(He starts toward closet.)*

ANN. Buster, what do you need hip boots for?

BUSTER *(matter-of-factly)*. To get your lemons.

ANN. You need hip boots to get lemons?

LESTER. It rained last night. Cellar's flooded. They're in the cellar.

ANN. Oh-hh.

BUSTER. I'll just be a minute.

ANN. Oh Buster, don't bother. I really don't need anything. Actually I should be going. My sister-in-law's expecting me at the house.

LESTER. You could call her.

ANN. I suppose I could but...

BUSTER. We got a lotta catchin' up to do. We can't let you get away this easy.

LESTER. You shouldn't be out driving in this weather anyway.

ANN. What weather? It is a little humid...

LESTER. Perfect tornado weather.

BUSTER. The radio said the weather's "just ripe" for a tornado, didn't it, Les?

LESTER *(looking daggers at BUSTER for stealing his line)*. Uh huh. Ripe.

BUSTER. Ripe conditions, that's what the radio said.

ANN. In that case I really had better get going, don't you think? I don't want to get caught. *(She smiles.)* It was good seeing you boys. *(She is in the doorway, about to leave.)*

LESTER. We'll be at the funeral.

BUSTER. You bet.

ANN. Well, good. We can have a better chance to visit then.

LESTER. Will Abner be there?

ANN *(after a stunned pause)*. Abner?

BUSTER. You know? Our brother Abner?

LESTER. The fellow you run off with while Buster was serving time and I was lying on my bed of pain in the hospital?

BUSTER. Right. Abner. Is he gonna be at the funeral?

ANN. I thought you knew. How could you not know?

BUSTER. Know what?

ANN. I wrote your mother when it happened. When I heard. She never told you?

LESTER. What?

BUSTER. Told us what?

ANN. Abner's been dead for many years. When we ran off, he joined the Army. He was going to make a career of it, but he died in Vietnam.

BUSTER. Jesus, no wonder he never wrote.

LESTER. You know, I always thought that was kind of funny, but I just thought he wasn't much of a letter writer.

ANN. My God. Why didn't your mother tell you?

LESTER. Yeah. I mean he was our baby brother. We woulda at least sent you a sympathy card.

BUSTER. She was prob'ly afraid we'd send more than that.

LESTER. Like what? Flowers? That can get pretty pricey.

BUSTER. I bet Ma was afraid it'd start up all over. If you 'n me'd known Ann was free, we mighta started up all over.

ANN. My God.

BUSTER. I bet that's the way her mind worked.

LESTER. She was pretty pissed about what happened, Bus going to prison and all.

ANN. I can imagine. And then Abner ran off with me...

LESTER. She did used to call you "that woman."

ANN. I just can't believe she didn't tell you. *(Enough with the mourning. BUSTER is a man with a mission.)*

BUSTER. So. You married again or what?

ANN. You know, I think I could use that lemonade. Bus, would you mind?

BUSTER. Mind? Hell no. *(He walks over to the closet for his hip boots; whips them out then quickly slams the door to avoid an avalanche.)*

LESTER. Won't you have a seat, Ann?

BUSTER. Yeah, honey, make yourself comfortable.

LESTER. Make yourself to home.

BUSTER. Hell yes. After all, alla this coulda been yours.

ANN. Oh my.

SCENE THREE

AT RISE: *A bit later. ANN, LESTER, and BUSTER—still in his hip boots, for that masculine appeal—are sitting drinking lemonade.*

ANN. You're right. It is better with a little whiskey. *(BUSTER winks at LESTER. LESTER scowls.)*

BUSTER. That's the way our Ma always made it.

ANN. She's gone now, isn't she?

LESTER. Yes, m'am. She keeled over weeding potatoes one day. Just keeled over dead.

ANN. That's a nice way to go.

LESTER. Her mind was starting to slip and she hated that. She always liked being one up on people. So it was prob'ly good for her she went when she did.

BUSTER *(nods)*. Dyin' in her potatoes was the best thing for her really.

ANN. My brother died in front of his television set.

BUSTER. Well, there's nothin' wrong with that.

ANN. His wife blames it on cable.

LESTER. More lemonade, Ann?

ANN. Thank you, Les, but I've still got half a glass. And I do have to be going soon. I really do.

BUSTER. Good ole Ma.

ANN. She was quite a character all right.

BUSTER. Her last few years she was on this artsy fartsy kick. She thought we all oughta take up some American craft, so it wouldn't get lost. She herself weaved throw rugs outa plastic bread sacks.

ANN. Now that *is* a lost art.

BUSTER. Whenever I buy a bagga Wonder Bread I always thinka Ma.

LESTER. I made these back scratchers outa corn cobs. *(He reaches for one—it's basically an old dried corn cob stuck on a stick—and proudly demonstrates.)* All lengths.

ANN. How about you, Bus? What did you make?

BUSTER *(pointing with pride at a large wooden mushroom sculpted from a block of wood)*. Chain saw sculpture.

ANN. My God, I never would've pictured you boys for artists.

LESTER. Still waters run deep.

BUSTER. I shoulda kept at that. There's good money in chain saw art.

LESTER. Bus made one for Ma's grave. It's supposed to be a squirrel.

BUSTER. But I'm better at mushrooms.

ANN. Well, it's the thought that counts.

BUSTER. That's what I told Les.

LESTER. I wonder what the weather's doing out there.

BUSTER. Well, get up off your ass 'n' look.

ANN. Is it getting dark yet? *(She is trying to see out an extremely dirty window.)* I don't want to be on the road after dark, especially after all this lemonade.

LESTER. It's still plenty light out. That window's just dirty. Bus, you ever gonna wash that window?

BUSTER. You're the one sits inside all day while I work this place. You could wash it yourself.

LESTER. You know how hard it is for me to do heavy labor—

BUSTER *(mutters)*. Heavy labor.

LESTER. —since you—since I was laid up.

BUSTER *(to ANN)*. He's never gonna let me live that down.

ANN. Well, you did put him in intensive care.

BUSTER. I did not. I just put him in the hospital. He's never been in no intensive care in his life. He tell you that?

ANN. Bus, I was there.

BUSTER. Well, I was in prison for two years, you think that was pleasant? 'Specially when I got out 'n' heard the news that you'd run off with Abner. I shoulda shot *him*.

ANN. Buster, I didn't want you to shoot *anybody*. Did you really think I'd be waiting for you after all that happened?

BUSTER. I didn't think you'd be gone.

LESTER. With Abner.

ANN. Don't look at me like that, Lester. You didn't own me. Neither of you did.

LESTER. I took a bullet for you. I took four bullets for you.

ANN. Les, this isn't "Gunsmoke."

BUSTER. Our own baby brother.

ANN. Well, he was sweet to me. Abner never came on strong. It started out he was just trying to be my friend. He knew how bad I felt. But then one night we were out for a drive, and we just never came back.

BUSTER. I could never understand it, how you could just leave with him. I was lots more handsome an' Les—Les worshiped the ground you spat on.

ANN. I liked both of you a lot. *(Brief pause as she eyes each of them, and they eye her back. There's still fire in those embers.)* But Abner was just so sweet.

BUSTER. Sweet my ass. He never woulda even tried it if Les 'n' me hadn't been outa circulation.

ANN. Abner was more than just available; he was a pleasure to be with.

LESTER. And we weren't?!

BUSTER. I picked up on that, too, Les.

ANN. The whole two years we were married, he was a pleasure to be with.

LESTER *(to BUSTER)*. He was "a pleasure to be with."

BUSTER. Unlike you'n me who're dogshit.

ANN *(refusing to be drawn into their mutterings, waxing poetic).* I remember the summer before he left for Vietnam we spent a weekend in Chicago. It was just a beautiful July night and we went to listen to waltz music in the park. There was a live orchestra playing. Night was coming on. The city was lighting up all around us. Oh, it was just like a movie. We were lying on the grass, sipping Dr. Peppers, listening to the music, people sitting on the grass all around us when all to once Abner stood up and pulled me to my feet—gentle like a man will when he's got nothing to prove—and we waltzed. There was nobody dancing but us, just us waltzing in the night with that whole city spread out all around us. That was really something. Oh my, that was something. I was lost when he died.

BUSTER *(to LESTER).* I hate that sensitive shit.

LESTER. Well, see where not being sensitive's got us; living here alone like two old maids.

BUSTER. Yeah but we're still kickin'. Abner's waltzed his last waltz.

ANN. I miss him. It's been years and years and I still miss him.

BUSTER. There's other fish in the sea, Ann. You shouldn't let yourself go to waste.

ANN. Well, I almost did get married again.

BUSTER. Oh yeah, who? We got some brother somewhere we don't know anything about?

ANN. I was dating this fellow I thought was Canadian, only it turns out he was Jewish. He had to cancel a date one day, because he hadn't realized it was Yom Kippur. *(ANN should mangle the pronunciation of this—Yon Kipper.)* Well, I'd always thought that was a Canadian holiday, so naturally I just assumed he was Canadian. *(LESTER and BUSTER nod encouragingly. They probably thought Yom*

Kippur was a Canadian national holiday too.) It was Christmastime when he got to talking about Hanukkah coming up that I caught on. Even *I* know Hanukkah's not a Canadian holiday, because I've seen "The Diary of Anne Frank" at least ten times, and it always just makes me cry when they sing the Hanukkah song all quiet so the Nazis won't find them only they do anyway. *(ANN softly sings "Oh, Hanukkah, oh, Hanukkah" to the tune of "Oh, Christmas Tree.")*

BUSTER. Dirty bastards.

LESTER. Isn't Shelley Winters in that movie? She really rubs me the wrong way.

BUSTER. Don't you wish.

ANN. Irv was pretty disgusted when he heard I thought Yom Kippur was a Canadian holiday. He took it personally. He said, "Where the hell did you grow up? Weren't there any Jews?" Well, you know there weren't. What Jewish person in his right mind would want to live up here with all these Baptists? They'll cut you dead if you're a Lutheran.

LESTER. After Bus shot me, they preached a whole sermon against our family. I thought that was pretty small. Singling out people who've already had kind of a bad year.

BUSTER. Hell, you'd think there was somethin' wrong with us, the way they acted. It coulda happened to anybody.

ANN. That relationship didn't pan out. Irv eventually married some woman who took tickets at a movie theater. I guess she was more refined.

BUSTER. So you yourself never remarried, right?

ANN. Right.

BUSTER. How about another lemonade? *(Reaches for the whiskey.)*

ANN. Thanks, Bus, but I really should be leaving if I'm going to have a chance for one last look at Al.

BUSTER. He prob'ly don't look any better dead.

LESTER. Annie, will you be staying around for a few days? You know, visit with his family, see the sights? There's a new sewage treatment plant since you left.

ANN. That's very tempting, Les, but I plan to head back to Indianapolis right after the funeral.

BUSTER. That's in Indiana, right?

ANN. Yes, I moved there after Abner passed on. I wanted to stay in the Midwest, but I couldn't bring myself to come back up here. And I'd always wanted to live in a state capital.

LESTER. What in the world do you do in a big city like that?

ANN. Oh, I work.

LESTER. What at?

ANN. Oh, it's just a job. Nothing special.

BUSTER. I'd never know how to even go about gettin' a job in the city. I asked this guy I was sharin' a cell with who was from Detroit, an' he said he'd never figured it out either.

LESTER. I bet you work in some nice store or office, don't you? All dressed up pretty?

ANN *(we can see she's uncomfortable)*. Actually, it's a phone job.

BUSTER. You got a job where you just talk on the phone?

LESTER. You mean you sell prescriptions to *Life* or something? That kinda phone job?

ANN. No. Look, I really should get going.

LESTER *(to BUSTER)*. What do you suppose she does?

BUSTER. Got me. Hey, I know; I got it. Ann, do you work for the phone company?

ANN. That's a funny thought.

BUSTER. What's funny about it? You said you work a phone. I don't think it was such a bad guess.

LESTER. I don't think it was.

ANN. That's right. Gang up on me. *(She is hunting up her purse, then hunting in it for her car keys.)*

BUSTER. She isn't gonna tell us, Les.

LESTER. Well, I guess she doesn't have to if she doesn't want to. It's her business. *(He's trying to be casual, but he can't hold it in. He's burning to know.)* But what else can you do over the phone? This is going to bother me all night. I'm not going to get a wink of sleep—sleep I desperately need—because this is going to eat away at me.

BUSTER. Ann, this is eatin' away at Lester.

ANN *(with finality)*. Too bad.

LESTER. If you don't sell *Life*, do you sell something else?

ANN *(after a brief pause)*. Sort of. Lester, please, trust me. You really don't want to know.

BUSTER. You sell swampland in Florida, or somethin'?

ANN. Dammit, you two never change. You always just push me too far.

LESTER. We're just curious.

ANN. It is none of your damn business.

BUSTER. Must be pretty bad.

ANN. Buster.

LESTER. We'd tell you what we do.

ANN. I know what you do.

BUSTER. Well yeah, but that's because we don't make it a secret.

LESTER. She doesn't know all we do.

BUSTER. Lester...

LESTER. Well, we can't tell her to spill her guts then hold out on her. That wouldn't be right.

ANN. I saw some marijuana growing out of your beanfield when I drove up. You really ought to grow marijuana in taller fields. It kind of stands out from the beans.

BUSTER. I give up.

LESTER. Do you sell insurance or vegetable slicers?

ANN. You aren't going to let this rest are you, Les?

LESTER. I'd just like to know.

ANN. Will you let me alone, will you please let me go and not dog me anymore if I tell you?

LESTER. Well sure.

ANN. You won't dwell on it?

LESTER. I never dwell.

ANN. Buster?

BUSTER. I already washed my hands of this.

ANN. You have to promise me, Lester. You'll let this drop. You won't drive me crazy when I tell you?

LESTER. Sure.

ANN. You promise?

LESTER. I promise, Annie.

ANN. I—make naughty phone calls.

BUSTER *(ears perking up)*. What's that?

ANN. I work through this service. Men—clients—pay me to talk to them over the phone.

LESTER. Clients?

ANN. It's easy work really. I can handle twenty or thirty calls in a day *and* clean my apartment. I have one of those cordless phones—

LESTER. Clients?!

ANN. I just call them and we talk through—well, whatever they want, their fantasies—till they're *(Brief pause.)* finished.

LESTER. Oh, Ann.

BUSTER. So what do you say?

ANN. Bus!

BUSTER. You'll talk dirt to total strangers but not to us, after all we've meant to you?

LESTER. Ann, why do you do it, oh why?

ANN. Lester, it pays the bills. And, well, it *is* safe sex. And because I'm good at it. I have a natural flare. And a lively imagination. The men who ask for me like me because I don't sound like some sexy centerfold. I could be their sister or their mother.

LESTER. Oh God.

ANN. Sometimes they want to pretend I am.

LESTER. Oh my God.

ANN. Les, don't look at me that way. You promised.

LESTER. How could you?

ANN. I got ten thousand dollars from the Army and twenty from Al for my share of the farm. When that ran out it was either this or Woolworth's. And I have bad ankles.

BUSTER. This tops it all.

LESTER. Our sweet Ann...

ANN. Don't act snotty about this, Lester. You're just the kind of guys who call me.

LESTER. I never would do that.

BUSTER. I would. I didn't even know there were such things. No wonder people live in cities.

LESTER. Oh, the things you've heard. And said. (To ANN.) You're practically a—a—*(He's leading up to the word "prostitute.")*

ANN. Lester, don't you dare.

LESTER. Practically.

BUSTER. You make a good living, huh?

ANN. Very respectable. I put a little aside for my retirement. It's not a profession that's covered by Social Security.

LESTER. God. *(He lapses into something resembling suspended animation or a catatonic state for a bit.)*

BUSTER. Lester, will you put a lid on it?! He acts like this about the dope I got growin' out in our beanfield. You'd think I was sellin' it over to the grade school. I don't sell to nobody under sixteen.

ANN. It's one reason I never came home to visit. Al used to tell me I'd burn in hell for it every chance he got, even in birthday cards. "Happy birthday, sister. I'm real sorry you're going to spend Eternity burning in the fiery furnace. Your loving brother, Al."

BUSTER. Why the hell'd you tell him in the first place? Why didn't you lie?

ANN. And tell him what? I bought that nice car and rent a two bedroom apartment clerking for Woolworth's?

BUSTER. Shit, he mighta bought it. Lotsa times people are so grateful you aren't tellin' 'em the truth they'll buy anything. Take Les. Look at him. If you'd told him you sell encyclopedias over the phone, he'd be the most grateful man alive.

ANN. Instead I've ruined his rosy little picture of me. Well, fine. It deserved to be ruined. I don't want to be worshipped. I never did.

BUSTER. We can't help it, honey, we're still just crazy about you. You know, you've kept yourself up real nice, Ann.

ANN. You don't look too bad yourself, Bus.

LESTER. Ann?

BUSTER *(growls)*. Great timing, Les, you asshole.

LESTER. Ann?

ANN. What?

LESTER. I'm sorry if I was rude.

ANN. That's all right.

LESTER. It's just not something I expected to hear. Not in a million years.

BUSTER. Real smooth, Les.

LESTER. But it's not my place to judge.

ANN. Exactly.

LESTER. God'll judge.

ANN. Lester, shut up.

LESTER. Ma wouldn't be a bit surprised.

BUSTER. Les, shut up!

ANN. Thanks, Bus.

BUSTER. I'd still like to hear what you tell those guys.

ANN. Buster! *(She punches him in the shoulder, but it's a playful punch—foreplay?)*

BUSTER. I could use another lemonade—maybe a beer. How about it, Ann? A nice cold one?

ANN. I've really got to go. Now. Right this minute. *(She rises.)* There, I'm up. You know, I've enjoyed this. Visiting with you boys. We never could do this before.

BUSTER. You could stay the night. You could stay in Ma's room. It's upstairs just like she left it with her jar of bag-balm on the dresser, her men's pajamas hangin' on the door. You could sleep there, Ann. You got my word, we'd be gentlemen.

ANN. Since when have you ever been a gentleman? *(Erotically charged moment. LESTER has moved over to the screen door to hold it open for ANN. He now stands gaping out at the weather.)*

LESTER. Geez, look at the sky. You don't want to go out in that.

ANN. I think I'd better. *(More steamy eye contact with BUSTER, then she moves to go.)*

LESTER. Bus, turn on the radio. Tune in a weather report.

BUSTER *(sardonically)*. Sure, Les.

LESTER. Buster, I mean it. Look at the sky if you don't believe me.

BUSTER *(approaching the door)*. Humor him, that's what Ma always said. Anything to make you happy, Lester. *(BUSTER sees the sky.)* Jesus! Look at that sky!

LESTER. I told you it was tornado weather. Maybe you'll learn to listen to me.

BUSTER. Shut up, Les.

ANN. Is that a train?

LESTER. Train? What train?

ANN. Listen. *(Slight pause.)* Don't you hear it?

BUSTER. Oh, Jesus Jesus.

LESTER. They pulled up the tracks. That's no train, that's a tornado headed straight for this house!

BUSTER. Jesus.

LESTER. What do we do what do we do?

ANN. The cellar!

LESTER. The cellar!

BUSTER. Okay by me, but don't forget the rats. *(Running to open the cellar door. The wind is visibly/audibly picking up outside.)*

ANN. Les, open the windows! The house will go if you don't!

BUSTER *(pulling aside the rug covering the trapdoor)*. Yeah, Les, open the windows!

LESTER. YOU open the windows. *(He's crawling under the table.)*

BUSTER *(pulling open the trapdoor that leads to the cellar)*. Goddammit, I'm busy!

LESTER. Well, so am I!

ANN *(hurrying around throwing open windows suddenly thinks)*. My car! *(The wind/train is coming closer.)*

BUSTER. Forget your car, come on! *(He gestures for her to come, jumps down a step. The stairs collapse beneath him; he clings to the opening.)*

ANN. Buster! Hold on! *(She runs to help him.)*

LESTER. I told you to fix those stairs.

BUSTER *(through gritted teeth, pulling himself out of the hole)*. I don't wanna hear it! *(ANN and BUSTER finally manage to pull him out of the hole in the floor; they slam the trapdoor shut. The wind is tearing at the house. The wind slams the door open. BUSTER lunges against the wind to close the door, but it won't close.)*

ANN. Buster, get away from the windows!

BUSTER *(mesmerized for a moment, staring out into the yard, into the tornado)*. There goes Ray's lawnmower.

ANN. Buster, get down! *(She drags him away just as a chicken is blown into his face.)*

BUSTER. Shit!

LESTER *(moaning)*. Oh my God, it's killing my chickens. *(BUSTER and ANN huddle; LESTER is under the table. The wind howls; pictures and dodads fall from the walls, ceiling plaster crashes to the floor.)*

BUSTER. We're gonna die!

ANN. Shut up, Buster!

LESTER. Oh God oh God oh God. *(We hear a loud crash, wood bending and wrenching.)*

BUSTER. Jeee-sus!

LESTER *(to BUSTER)*. I told you conditions were ripe.

BUSTER *(to LESTER)*. If this tornado don't kill you, I will!

ANN. Ohmygod! *(Blackout.)*

INTERMISSION—END ACT ONE

ACT TWO

AT RISE: *Through the dim, dust-filled light we can see that the house is an even worse mess than it is normally. Furniture, pots and pans, everything is helter-skelter. The closet door has blown open and there's an avalanche spilling from it including the chain saw. We can see BUSTER and ANN sprawled in a heap together, but we can't pick LESTER out from the rest of the debris. BUSTER stirs, blinks, looks down at the unconscious ANN. Perhaps he fumbles in his pocket for his lighter and lights it to see her better.*

BUSTER. Ann? Annie, are you all right? Oh please, wake up. *(He shakes her a little, caresses her cheek.)* Oh, Ann, don't be dead. *(ANN stirs.)* Ann? Annie? Anybody home?

ANN *(eyes open)*. Oh my, do I ache. What happened? *(Focusing.)* Dear God, look at this place. *(She remembers.)* The tornado.

BUSTER. Hell, we're lucky to be alive. That sucker hit us right between the eyes.

ANN. Where's Lester?

BUSTER. Oh oh.

ANN. I don't see him. Lester?

BUSTER. Oh shit. Les!

ANN. Lester!

BUSTER. Lester, where are you?!

ANN. Bus, over there! *(LESTER is lying on the floor, the mushroom sculpture rammed into his chest.)*

BUSTER. Oh dear Lord, my mushroom killed him.

ANN. Oh, Lester.

BUSTER *(hurls the mushroom aside)*. I can't tell if he's breathin'. Oh Jesus, Ann. *(ANN drops to her knees beside LESTER and proceeds to perform CPR.)*

ANN *(shakes his shoulder, barks)*. Lester, Lester, are you okay?! Les? *(She tilts his head by the chin and places her ear near his mouth to listen for air and watch his chest for movement. Nothing. She pinches his nose, blows a couple of breaths of air in his mouth, checks his pulse.)* There's a pulse! Buster, call 911. *(BUSTER hurries to phone. The receiver is imbedded in a dead chicken.)*

BUSTER. Geez. *(He pulls the phone from the chicken, listens for a dial tone. The cord is obviously hanging loose from the wall, but he doesn't notice.)* Hello hello. *(Blows a chicken feather out of his mouth.)* Phone's dead. *(ANN pinches LESTER's nose, forms a seal on his mouth with hers, starts breathing into him. LESTER's arms rise and wrap around her. He kisses her until she gets a knee into him.)*

ANN. Goddammit, Lester!

LESTER. Ouch!

BUSTER. He's alive!

ANN. He's alive all right. *(She is glowering at LESTER.)*

LESTER. Oh, I hurt all over.

ANN. Lester, if you *ever* try that again, you are really going to hurt.

LESTER. What? What did I do? Oh God, everything's going black again.

ANN. Tell somebody who cares.

LESTER. I was flying, just like Peter Pan only there weren't any wires. Everything in the room was flying. Suddenly the wind stopped, and we all fell down. Oh, I can feel every bullet wound. They never really heal, you know.

ANN *(not at all kindly)*. Isn't it just amazing you're alive.

BUSTER. What a mess. I don't even wanna look outside. *(But he does look out the doorway—there's no longer a door.)* Oh boy.

ANN. Bad?

LESTER. Not my chickens!

BUSTER. Yard's full of 'em. An' Ann's car's stickin' outa the side of the barn, twenty feet off the ground.

LESTER *(perks up)*. Does that mean she'll be staying the night?

ANN. I am never performing CPR on anyone ever again. People can drop dead at my feet and I'll just step right over them.

LESTER. Was it that bad?

ANN. Mister, you were out of line.

LESTER. I couldn't help it. It wasn't my fault. I was delirious. Air sick. I've got a cold. Besides, you kissed me first.

ANN. I wasn't kissing you, Lester. I was performing CPR.

LESTER. Same difference.

BUSTER. Les, you're a sad case.

ANN. Lester, I used to like you because you didn't pull crap like that. You always asked first.

LESTER. I'm sorry, Ann.

ANN. You should be.

BUSTER. You know, it's gonna get dark soon. We got any candles? Hey you, Les, where do we keep the candles?

LESTER. There's some little stubby ones in the kitchen, in with the silverware. And Ma had some tall fancy ones in her closet upstairs.

BUSTER. I'm gonna run upstairs an' hunt those up. Gonna be a long night. *(He starts up the stairs then pauses and looks at LESTER who is still on the floor.)* Les, do you need help gettin' up?

LESTER. Thank you, but I'm happy on the floor.

BUSTER. You would be. *(He exits up the stairs.)*

ANN *(rummaging in the kitchen drawers)*. There aren't any candles in here, Les.

LESTER. Check the refrigerator.

ANN. The refrigerator?

LESTER. Ma always said in case of fire, keep your valuables in the freezer.

ANN. Les, I think she meant your will, not your *(She dips a hand into the freezer.)* underwear. *(She gingerly holds up a frigid pair of undershorts.)*

LESTER. They're Buster's. We can't afford air conditioning.

ANN *(gingerly picking through the contents of the kitchen)*. A lantern. Great. Things are looking up.

(BUSTER enters, empty-handed.)

LESTER. Couldn't you find Ma's candles?

BUSTER. Couldn't find the upstairs.

LESTER. What?! *(BUSTER's words sinking in, LESTER starts struggling to his feet.)*

BUSTER. Ma's room, my moosehead, the bathroom, it's all gone. I can't even see where it landed. Could be in the next county by now. But it's gone. Long gone. Tore right off. Dad added that floor on forty years ago. It's gone now. Jesus.

LESTER. That's not right. That can't be right. You got a screw loose. *(Pounding his leg to get the circulation moving, hurriedly limps to the stairs.)*

BUSTER. I hope I *am* hallucinatin'—but I'm not. It's gone. Boy, I'm gonna miss that moosehead. He had a lotta sentimental value. I won him at poker.

ANN. Sorry, Bus.

LESTER. It can't be gone. You can't just lose an upstairs, just like that. *(He exits up the stairs.)*

BUSTER. Lookit that bastard move. The part about the bathroom really got to him. Geez, can you believe this?

ANN *(lights lamp and sets it down)*. My.

BUSTER *(looks at her in the lamplight, forgets the upstairs)*. You look real pretty in lamplight.

ANN. I look like a wreck. I can feel my hair sticking straight up.

BUSTER. Well, whose wouldn't? *(They look around at the debris.)* Les is really gonna miss that bathroom. *(He says it in all seriousness, but after a brief pause ANN breaks into explosive laughter.)* Hey, I'm serious. That was his favorite room in the house.

ANN. Oh God. *(Wiping her eyes.)* It's all just so—Funny.

BUSTER. What a mess. I wonder if the radio works. Should. It's a battery. *(The radio is attached to a car battery with jumper cables.)*

ANN. Why don't you try it?

BUSTER. Yeah, why don't I try it? *(After a smoldering look passes between them, BUSTER turns on the radio.)*

RADIO ANNOUNCER. ...a path of devastation across two counties. Rescue workers are still trying to determine if any human lives have been lost. We do know there has been a price paid in the lives of our poultry. And apparently several of our dear departed departed once again when this twister blew away Twinings Funeral Home. If any of these folks turn up in your backyard, we'd appreciate a call...

ANN. Oh dear. Al hated to fly.

BUSTER. Poor bastard. Got killed twice. *(Flipping the dial.)* Well, at least we aren't dead. *(BUSTER stops dialing. An old instrumental is playing.)*

ANN. Abner loved that song. *(BUSTER extends a hand in as courtly a manner as he can manage.)*

BUSTER. How about it, Ann?

ANN. You want to dance in the middle of a tornado?

BUSTER. Well, I don't waltz and I'm no polka king, but I do promise to stay off your toes.

ANN. Well, why not? Why the hell not? *(They move into each other's arms, clumsy and shy at first.)* Only you would want to dance after a tornado.

BUSTER. Nerves of steel. Hell, we're alive. That's somethin' to dance about.

ANN. You're right. It is. *(They dance.)*

BUSTER. You know, I haven't done this in a long time.

ANN. Neither have I.

BUSTER. I had a few dances after you left, but it was never the same.

ANN. We did have some good times.

BUSTER. I sure missed you when you left.

ANN. But it was for the best. It was. You and Lester would've killed each other.

BUSTER. What'd you ever see in him?

ANN. I could push Lester around. You'd push me, I'd push Les—with Abner there was kind of a nice balance.

BUSTER. You were the prettiest girl in the county.

ANN. You're so full of it.

BUSTER. You were. Still are. I thought it was a miracle you'd look at any of us twice.

ANN. Do you remember me when I was a little girl, up till freshman year of high school?

BUSTER *(thinks, shakes his head)*. Sorry. Guess I was too busy playin' ball.

ANN. I was very fat.

BUSTER. Oh yeah? I don't remember.

ANN. That's because you never hollered anything at me. All the other boys in school did. Mean, rotten things. But not you. Or Les or Abner. Never. Not once. When I was fourteen, my mother dieted me to within an inch of my life. Suddenly boys were coming out of the woodwork—boys who'd called me fatso and lardass a year ago—they were all over me like flies in shit. They had a very short memory, but I didn't. If they didn't want me when I was fat, I didn't want them because I got skinny. But I didn't have any bad memories of you boys. You were cordial. And you never went out of your way to hurt me. I appreciated it.

BUSTER. Well, you know our mom weighed about three fifty. We never woulda dreameda givin' a fat kid a hard time. Now retards were another matter.

ANN. Lucky I wasn't retarded.

BUSTER. You're still the prettiest girl in the county.

(They lock gazes. BUSTER leans down to kiss ANN. As they're kissing, LESTER enters, walking slowly down the stairs. He's holding a toilet seat to his chest, cradling it, as he takes the steps one at a time. He doesn't notice what BUSTER and ANN are up to.)

LESTER. Mom's room. My medicine chest. Your magazines. Gone. This was all there was left. How are we gonna live without a bathroom?

BUSTER *(picks up a metal cooking pot)*. Here you go, Les. Here's a pot to piss in. Where's your pioneer spirit?

LESTER. I just sat up there, looking up at the sky.

ANN. We wondered what had become of you.

BUSTER. Yeah, we were real concerned.

LESTER. So what's been going on down here?

ANN *(casually)*. Oh, we've just been dancing. *(Extending her arms toward LESTER.)* How about a spin, Les?

LESTER. No, thank you. I can't. Not with my bad leg. *(But he looks at her longingly.)*

ANN. Come on, Lester. I'll lead.

BUSTER. I'll hold your seat. *(LESTER hates to give it up, but he hands the toilet seat to BUSTER and steps into ANN's arms. They dance with her leading. BUSTER picks up the dead chicken lying next to the phone.)* Think it'd be safe to eat her? It's way past suppertime.

LESTER *(dancing, eyes closed, entranced)*. Buster, you know how I feel about my chickens.

ANN. Lester, forget about your chickens. *(She dips LESTER.)*

LESTER *(startled, but he dips)*. Hey!

SCENE TWO

AT RISE: *The dark is relieved by candles, perhaps a flashlight on end, or a lantern. ANN, LESTER, and BUSTER sit with beer bottles in hand.*

BUSTER *(finally)*. What the hell did we do before TV?

LESTER. What the hell did we do before Dad put in a bathroom?

BUSTER. Good bologna sandwiches, Les. My compliments to the chef.

ANN. I feel so sad for my car.

BUSTER. Gonna be a helluva trick to get it down outa the side of the barn. Maybe we should just leave it there. Charge admission.

ANN. How many did the radio say were killed?

BUSTER. Two.

LESTER. And all my chickens. What am I gonna do now for companionship?

BUSTER. Jesus, Les.

LESTER. They loved me like a mother. I'd limp out into the yard and call to them, and they'd cackle up at me just so bright and cheerful. *(He mimes throwing feed then mimics the chickens cackling.)*

BUSTER. Les, cut it out.

LESTER. They all had their own individual little voices. Daisy had this little catch in her cackle. *(He mimics a chicken with a catch in her cackle.)*

ANN. Well, they're in heaven now, Lester. They're at peace with God. *(These people really have been drinking!)*

LESTER. You think?

ANN. Oh, absolutely.

LESTER. That makes me feel better.

BUSTER. If my cash crop came through this okay, we can harvest a few ounces and buy you some new ones.

LESTER. Thank you, Bus. My chickens can't really be replaced—not in my heart of hearts—but it's sweet of you to offer.

BUSTER. Don't mention it.

ANN. I wonder if they ever found Al.

BUSTER. Ole brother Al may be in Kansas by now.

ANN. You know, next to you shooting Les this is the most exciting thing that's ever happened to me in my entire life.

LESTER. What about Abner?

ANN. He was so sweet to be with and I loved him dearly, but I just couldn't in all honesty call Abner exciting. He was too nice to be exciting.

LESTER. So where's he buried?

ANN. There was so little left he was cremated. I carry him with me.

BUSTER. You're shittin' me.

ANN. No, really.

BUSTER. Ann, don'tcha think that's kinda sick?

LESTER. I'd like to see. Can I see?

BUSTER *(to LESTER)*. Kissass.

LESTER. He was our brother. I'd like to see his remains.

BUSTER. So stick your head in the stove. We got ashes in there.

ANN *(rummaging in her purse)*. He's in here somewhere.

LESTER. You've carried him with you all this time?

ANN. Um hmm. *(Rummaging.)* Until—To tell the truth I've been waiting for a chance to bury him here. Find a nice tree where not too many dogs "go."...Here. *(She has a silver cylinder, screws it out and back.)* No, that's my lipstick.

LESTER. Ann...

ANN *(rummaging)*. I can't believe this...*(Preoccupied.)* What, Les?

LESTER *(watching the lipstick)*. Remember that time...

BUSTER. That time what?

LESTER. This is private.

BUSTER. No, it's not.

ANN. Let's not dig up the past. Oh, thank God, here he is. *(She holds up a silver cylinder.)* This is all there was left. Part of a shoulder blade and one toe. They I.D.'d him from the toeprint.

LESTER *(eyes the cylinder)*. That's Abner?

ANN. Dear, sweet…

BUSTER. …dull…

ANN. Abner.

LESTER *(softly and sincerely)*. Welcome home, Ab.

BUSTER. You are one sick sonofabitch.

LESTER. Tomorrow let's have a service and bury him. Do we bury him or spread him? We can set out one of your mushrooms to mark the spot.

ANN *(looking at LESTER, misty-eyed)*. He'd like that.

LESTER. Bus, do you think you could bring in some wood? I'm getting kind of chilly.

BUSTER. What the hell'd you do with that wood I got you this morning?

LESTER. It's prob'ly wherever the upstairs is. And my chickens. Oh dear God, we've got to bury them too.

BUSTER. Sure, Les. I'll make 'em each a little egg-shaped headstone an' we'll bury 'em right next to Abner, so he won't be lonesome. Him 'n' Daisy can cluck at each other all day long.

LESTER. Don't make jokes about Daisy. She was my favorite chicken. *(He looks about ready to cry.)*

ANN. Bus, don't be mean to him. He's lost a lot today.

BUSTER. Well, so have I.

ANN. But you're stronger. *(LESTER smiles sneakily to himself then sighs melodramatically.)*

BUSTER. Christ. *(He starts to exit.)* I'll be right back, Lester. *(He exits to get the wood, muttering as he goes.)* I hope to hell the woodpile's still there. Took me several nights to steal all that wood…*(Exits.)*

LESTER. He just doesn't understand.

ANN. Buster's got a soft side, but he hates to show it.

LESTER. It's sure nice having you here, Ann. It was almost worth the mess.

ANN *(laughing)*. Well, thank you, Les, but I didn't bring the tornado.

LESTER. It felt like you did. It felt like a storm was in the house the minute you came. Maybe it was just a storm in my heart.

ANN. You can be quite a talker, Les.

LESTER. You bring out the poet in me.

ANN. That's sweet.

LESTER. Bus thinks I talk too much.

ANN. Well, that's his opinion.

LESTER. Do you think I talk too much, Ann?

ANN. Les, he's going to be back any minute.

LESTER. That lipstick reminded me, going in and going out, in and out. It reminded me of that time you let me. It was the high point of my life.

ANN. You acted like you were in church.

LESTER. That's just how it felt. Ann, was it so bad when I grabbed you? I was really out of it or I never would've done that. Really.

ANN. I just don't like being grabbed, Les. And I didn't expect it from you.

LESTER *(closing in)*. I think I was just crazed, because I was afraid it was going to be the only chance I'd ever get to touch you again. *(Erotically charged moment.)*

ANN. It looks like you were wrong.

LESTER. I still feel like I'm in church.

ANN. Well, start praying. Buster will be back any minute. *(LESTER leans toward her, lips puckered. ANN pulls him to her, kisses him. They kiss for a few seconds, pull apart.)*

LESTER. It's a lot better when you like it.

ANN. A lot. Oh God, where did the time go? *(Kisses him.)*

LESTER. You taste like bologna. *(He leans in, about to kiss her again.)*

(BUSTER enters with an armload of firewood.)

BUSTER. You whisperin' secrets to each other, or what?

LESTER. That's right, Buster. Or what. *(He smiles at ANN, steps away.)*

ANN *(to BUSTER)*. I'm surprised you could find any wood.

BUSTER. Well, it took me a couple minutes. *(He glowers.)* It don't look like you missed me.

LESTER. You're right. We didn't. *(BUSTER and LESTER glare at each other.)*

ANN. Time just melts away. *Bonnie and Clyde* is on at the drive-in and you two are all over me like lice.

LESTER. We dropped Betty Rhodes flat when we fell for you.

ANN. You were both dating Betty Rhodes before you started dating me? I never knew that. Have you two always liked the same girls?

BUSTER and LESTER *(in unison)*. Sure.

ANN. You never liked a girl that Lester didn't like? And the other way around? *(LESTER and BUSTER shake their heads, a bit mystified by the very idea.)*

BUSTER. We always been a close family.

LESTER. Didn't you and Al always want the same stuff when you were kids?

ANN. Well, sure—when we were kids. If he had a candy bar, I wanted it. And he was always stealing my lunch...

LESTER. That's how it starts. With a lunch.

BUSTER. That's just how we were. Put two identical hamburgers in front of us, we'd both want the same one.

ANN. Where did Abner fit in?

BUSTER. He didn't. He was too little. He maya wanted the same stuff we did, but he knew if we caught him makin' a grab for it we woulda beat the hell outa him. 'Course when it counted, we didn't catch him.

LESTER. Remember when we had our tonsils out?

BUSTER. Yeah, now there was a classic case. I was s'posed to go in to have my tonsils out. Well, we get to the doctor's office 'n' this asshole starts cryin' 'cause he wants his out too. Well, to shut him up the doctor takes a look down his throat.

LESTER. Mine needed taking out even worse than Buster's.

BUSTER. So in we went. Had 'em out the same day.

LESTER. I bled more than he did.

BUSTER. Anything I had he wanted. A frog, warts, you name it. Jesus, I'd half look at a girl an' he was in love. When I fell for you, Les was right there, breathin' down my neck.

LESTER. I noticed her first. I liked her when she was fat.

BUSTER. You did not, you lyin' sacka shit.

LESTER. Abner must've had his eye on you too.

BUSTER. Well, this time he shouldn't be much competition.

ANN. Oh God, I don't think I can live through another courtship.

LESTER. You could always just choose.

ANN. Choose? Are you kidding? Choose?! I'm more confused now than I was then. *(Steamy.)* And I still like you both.

LESTER. Well, *(Pause/thinks.)* we could share you.

BUSTER. Lester, you asshole, that's Communism.

ANN. I should never have come back.

LESTER. You could be with Buster on odd days and me even. Or we could go by the month.

BUSTER. Lester, shut up. Share her. Jesus.

LESTER. I got a right to talk, Buster. This concerns me too. You're so goddamn pushy.

BUSTER. *I'm* pushy? All you do is push me around. You do it in that weak, whiny tone of voice, but it's pushing. It is pushing.

LESTER. You were born mean.

BUSTER. You weasel.

ANN. Stop it.

LESTER. Don't you call me a weasel.

BUSTER. You just told me I was born mean. You think I haven't got feelings? You weasel.

ANN. Both of you stop this right now.

BUSTER. Maybe we could draw straws.

ANN. You are not drawing straws.

BUSTER. You got a better idea?

ANN. I think—I think I should leave. Bus, could you drive me to my sister-in-law's place?

BUSTER. I don't know as I got any gas.

ANN *(through gritted teeth)*. Find some.

LESTER. Please don't leave, Ann.

ANN. But I can't stay. How can I stay?

BUSTER. Les could always leave. Ma left the place to me. It's my place.

LESTER. You bastard.

BUSTER. She said Les never shoulda pressed charges against me, so she left me the place to try 'n' make up for the two years he stole offa me.

ANN. But Bus, you did shoot him.

BUSTER. Once! In the leg. I barely scratched him. He shot himself all those other places. He thought it'd get your attention. He said he just wanted to get your attention. *(Stunned silence.)*

LESTER. How could you tell her that? That was a family secret.

BUSTER. Well, she's family. Besides, it's been eatin' at my craw for years. *(To ANN.)* Ma was afraid they'd put him in the looney bin 'n' throw away the key if we told the truth.

LESTER. Why don't you just shoot me, Buster?

BUSTER. Nope. I learned my lesson. This psychological shit works a whole lot better. An' it don't land ya in prison.

LESTER. Since when were you ever afraid of a little prison? Come on, Buster, just kill me. You've as good as killed me already. Don't leave me still breathing.

BUSTER. All right! *(He strides to the closet and plucks a gun from the avalanche.)* Is this what you want?

ANN. Buster, no.

BUSTER. Is it? Is it, Les?

ANN. Buster—

BUSTER. You heard him. He wants me to shoot him.

ANN. Buster, no! *(BUSTER walks over to LESTER. A long, tension-filled moment, then he hands LESTER the gun.)*

BUSTER. Here. You're good at shootin' yourself. Kill yourself if you wanna, Lester. I'm not doin' it for ya.

LESTER *(hesitates then takes the gun)*. Is it loaded?

BUSTER. Of course, it's loaded. What good's a empty gun?

LESTER *(points gun at BUSTER)*. I shoulda shot *you* that first time. Insteada sending you to prison, I shoulda sent you to the marble orchard.

BUSTER. Jesus, Lester, don't point that thing at me. Les, don't point that at me.

ANN. Lester, give me the gun.

LESTER. How you like it, Bus? How you like having the gun pointing at you for a change?

BUSTER. I don't. Now just take it easy.

LESTER. You always said prison was worse than being shot. You still think that?

ANN. Lester, put down the gun.

BUSTER. Take it easy, Les.

LESTER. Take it easy? A tornado just blew away my bathroom and all my chickens and I'm supposed to take it easy? I came outa the hospital all those years ago lovesick, only to find out she'd run off with our baby brother who was the most boring human being on the face of the earth. I'm supposed to take it easy? I sit here freezing and you begrudge me a load of wood. Daisy's dead and there are rats in the cellar and I'm supposed to take it easy? You betrayed a family trust and made me look like a crazy man when I was just a man in love and I'm supposed to take it easy?! Goddammit, I'm tireda being easy and I'm tireda bein' taken! *(He points the gun at BUSTER.)*

BUSTER *(grabs up the chain saw)*. All right, go ahead! Shoot me! Shoot me, you weasel sonofabitch, but I'm takin' one of your legs with me. *(He roars the chain saw at LESTER.)*

LESTER. I'm going to shoot you, Buster. I'm going to shoot you dead! *(BUSTER revs the chain saw at him.)*

ANN *(her voice takes on a cold, firm, mother-like insistence)*. Lester, you put down that gun this instant. I mean it, Lester. Put it down. *(LESTER pauses, looks at her.)* Lester, did you hear me? *(He flexes his mouth, looks at her, looks at BUSTER, looks back at ANN.)* I don't want to have to tell you again. *(LESTER lets the gun droop, sighs, lays it down, walks away to sit by the Blaze Princess. He reaches for his blanket.)* The chain saw, Buster. Put it down now.

BUSTER *(sets it down, reverent)*. Is that the way you talk to those guys on the phone?

ANN. I have had it with you two. Had it! I don't mean anything to you. Not really. I don't mean any more to you than a pair of socks you both want. Or a frog. Or a pickup. Christ, you have two identical pickups sitting out there because neither of you can let the other get one up on him. I'm just a bone for a couple of old dogs to fight over.

LESTER. But you're a T-bone, Ann.

ANN. When I leave, you'll just go back to bickering about whatever the hell you two bicker about when I'm not around. Well, I'm sick of it. I want peace.

BUSTER. Jesus, haven't you had enough peace?

ANN. I've had enough excitement today to last me for a long time. *(Picking up her sweater and purse.)* Goodbye, boys. I'm walking to town. Alone.

BUSTER. I could drive you.

LESTER. Me too.

ANN. No, thank you.

LESTER. If they ever find Al's body, we'll see you at the funeral.

ANN. Oh, please don't come. Goodbye. *(Exits.)*

BUSTER. Shit.

LESTER. Is that all you can say? Buster, she's gone. We gotta stop her.

BUSTER. What do you want me to do? Buzz off one of her legs?

LESTER *(after a pause)*. I guess not.

BUSTER *(flashes to the gun incident)*. Jesus Christ, Lester, you almost shot me.

LESTER. Almost doesn't count.

BUSTER. You ever point another gun at me, you're gonna be one sorry sonofabitch.

LESTER *(wrapping himself further into the safety of his blanket)*. I won't. *(Moment of silence.)*

BUSTER. It's not fair.

LESTER. What?

BUSTER. Her comin' back only to leave.

LESTER. Who says life's fair? The yard's fulla dead chickens.

BUSTER. Too bad she had to look so good. That makes it harder.

LESTER. She tasted like bologna.

BUSTER. Oh, yeah? I thought she tasted like lemonade.

LESTER *(picking up the container that holds Abner's ashes)*. She forgot Abner. We'll have to bury him tomorrow.

BUSTER. Jesus, I forgot about him.

LESTER. We lost a lot today. I never even knew we had anything.

BUSTER. Lost a brother. Lost our girlfriend.

LESTER. Lost our bathroom.

BUSTER. Maybe Ray Bailey'll help me put a john in the back room. You got the seat.

LESTER *(looks out into the yard)*. Looks like his lawn mower blew over by the refrigerators. Oh, there's a chicken on it. I bet it's Mildred. God, she was a sweet-natured chicken.

BUSTER *(also looking out)*. Ann'll have to come back for her car. Or send a wrecker. She'll prob'ly just send a wrecker.

LESTER. We'll never see her again.

BUSTER. Yup.

LESTER. Well, at least we've got each other. *(A moment of nausea passes over their faces, but it is replaced by some genuine brotherly warmth.)*

BUSTER. You warm enough, Les? I can get you more wood.

LESTER. I'm fine. Fine as I'll ever be. Thanks for asking.

BUSTER. How's your cold?

LESTER. Worse.

BUSTER. Well, whose wouldn't be? Want a cup of coffee or anything? *(We hear steps and cackling from the porch.)* Hey, who's out there?! We got a gun!

ANN *(from outside)*. Jesus, don't I know it.

(She enters carrying a live chicken.)

ANN. Look what I found. I think she's been in the marijuana because she was walking in circles and just cackling up a storm.

BUSTER. Ann?

LESTER. Daisy? Oh, Daisy! *(The blanket drops from his shoulders as he limps to his beloved chicken.)* Oh Ann, how can I ever thank you? Oh, thank you.

BUSTER. That was real sweet of you to bring her back, Ann.

ANN. I always seem to be taking off, don't I? And it never lasts.

LESTER *(to ANN and BUSTER in wonder)*. She's alive.

BUSTER *(to ANN)*. I used to tell Ma she oughta get him a dog. People don't think it's so weird when somebody acts like that about a dog. But Ma was a chicken woman herself.

LESTER. Ann?

ANN. Lester?

LESTER. Are you back?

ANN. The boards over your drainage ditch were washed out, but I was determined to wade across. Only then I stopped, one shoe off, and asked myself where was I going? Everybody I care about, everybody who cares about me, even my car, you're all right here. So I turned around. I must be insane.

LESTER. Oh now, Ann, you're just as normal as me and Buster.

ANN. That's what scares me.

BUSTER. We do love you, Ann.

LESTER. We've spent our entire adult lives waiting for you to come back. We didn't even realize that's what we were doing until we saw you.

ANN. So can I gain two hundred pounds and then one day keel over in your potato patch?

BUSTER. Ann, if that'll make you happy, I'll buy you the Oreos.

LESTER. I'll take you to Ponderosa for their all-you-can-eat salad and dessert bar.

BUSTER. I'll take her. *(Stormy passions rise.)*

ANN. Why don't you both take me. *(A steamy pause followed by agreement. As the MEN rush to open the door for her.)*

LESTER. What was that?

BUSTER. What was what? *(Now we can hear it, growing closer and closer, louder and louder.)*

ANN. Oh no. I hear it too.

BUSTER. Holy shit.

LESTER. Oh, Daisy.

BUSTER. You know, Ann, you don't exactly bring a guy good luck. *(The house is shaking; the tornado is again at their door.)*

ANN. Buster, shut up.

LESTER. Here we go again!

CURTAIN—END OF PLAY

PRODUCTION NOTES

Because some audiences may find certain words and phrases in *RIPE CONDITIONS* offensive, we have provided a list of alternatives which you may choose to use. These alternatives are covered under the copyright for this play. No other changes in the script may be made:

ass	butt; hindquarters; duff
asshole	scum; dirty so-and-so
bastard	dirty so-and-so
Christ	cripes; hallelujah
Chrissakes	(for) cryin' out loud
dogshit	dog do-do; doggy-do
flies in shit	flies in a cow pasture
God	gosh; geez
Goddamn	gosh darn; hallelujah
Goddamnit	gosh darn it; gol-dang-it
hell	heck; heckfire
jackshit	dog do-do; a dead man risen
Jesus	geez; hallelujah
Jesus Christ	geez oh petes
kissass	teacher's pet
Oh, my God	good golly; dear heavens
shit	shoot
shittin' me	pullin' my leg
son of a bitch	son of a gun; son of a...

DIRECTOR'S NOTES